HIP-HOP

50 Cent

Ashanti

Beyoncé

Mary J. Blige

Chris Brown

Mariah Carey

Sean "Diddy" Combs

Dr. Dre

Missy Elliott

Eminem

Hip-Hop: A Short History

Jay-Z

Alicia Keys

LL Cool J

Ludacris

Nelly

Notorious B.I.G.

Queen Latifah

Reverend Run (Run-D.M.C.)

Will Smith

Snoop Dogg

Tupac

Usher

Kanye West

Pharrell Williams

Hip-Hop

Sean "Diddy" Combs

Kelly Wittmann

Mason Crest Publishers

Sean "Diddy" Combs

FRONTIS Influential hip-hop producer and rapper Sean "Diddy" Combs performs at the 2005 MTV Video Music Awards.

PRODUCED BY 21ST CENTURY PUBLISHING AND COMMUNICATIONS, INC.

MASON CREST PUBLISHERS INC.
370 Reed Road
Broomall, Pennsylvania 19008
(866)MCP-BOOK (toll free)
www.masoncrest.com

Printed in Malaysia.

First Printing

9 8 7 6 5 4 3 2 1

Library of Congress Cataloging-in-Publication Data

Wittmann, Kelly.
    Sean "Diddy" Combs / Kelly Wittmann.
       p. cm. — (Hip-hop)
    Includes bibliographical references and index.
    ISBN-13: 978-1-4222-0115-2
    ISBN-10: 1-4222-0115-5
    1. P. Diddy, 1970–   —Juvenile literature. 2. Rap musicians—United States—Biography—Juvenile literature. I. Title. II. Series.
    ML3930.P84W58 2007
    782.421649092—dc22
    [B]   2006011449

Contents

Hip-Hop Timeline   6

1 A Good Run   9

2 Inborn Ambition   15

3 Climbing the Ladder of Success   23

4 Trouble at the Top   33

5 Controversy and Charitable Works   45

Chronology   56

Accomplishments & Awards   58

Further Reading & Internet Resources   60

Glossary   61

Index   62

Picture Credits   64

About the Author   64

Hip-Hop Timeline

1974 Hip-hop pioneer Afrika Bambaataa organizes the Universal Zulu Nation.

1988 *Yo! MTV Raps* premieres on MTV.

1970s Hip-hop as a cultural movement begins in the Bronx, New York City.

1985 *Krush Groove,* a hip-hop film about Def Jam Recordings, is released featuring Run-D.M.C., Kurtis Blow, LL Cool J, and the Beastie Boys.

1970s DJ Kool Herc pioneers the use of breaks, isolations, and repeats using two turntables.

1979 The Sugarhill Gang's song "Rapper's Delight" is the first hip-hop single to go gold.

1986 Run-D.M.C. are the first rappers to appear on the cover of *Rolling Stone* magazine.

1970

1980

1988

1970s Break dancing emerges at parties and in public places in New York City.

1976 Grandmaster Flash & the Furious Five pioneer hip-hop MCing and freestyle battles.

1986 Beastie Boys' album *Licensed to Ill* is released and becomes the best-selling rap album of the 1980s.

1982 Afrika Bambaataa embarks on the first European hip-hop tour.

1988 Hip-hop music annual record sales reaches $100 million.

1970s Graffiti artist Vic pioneers tagging on subway trains in New York City.

1984 *Graffiti Rock,* the first hip-hop television program, premieres.

1993 Rapper Snoop Dogg's album *Doggystyle* is the first debut album to hit the music charts at number one.

2006 Queen Latifah becomes the first hip-hop artist to receive a star on the Hollywood Walk of Fame.

1989 DJ Jazzy Jeff & The Fresh Prince become the first hip-hop artists to win a Grammy Award.

2003 Rapper Eminem becomes the first hip-hop artist to win an Academy Award.

2005 Hip-hop artist Kanye West appears on the cover of *Time* magazine.

1989 Rap is added as a new category to the *Billboard* charts.

1997 East Coast rapper Notorious B.I.G. (aka Biggie Smalls) is murdered.

2004 First National Hip-Hop Political Convention is held in Newark, New Jersey.

1989   2000   2006

1990s Hip-hop emerges in Europe.

1996 West Coast rapper Tupac Shakur is shot and killed.

2005 Rapper Will Smith opens the Philadelphia Live 8 concert as part of 10 simultaneous concerts held worldwide to bring attention to the extreme poverty in Africa.

1989 First gangsta rap album, *Straight Outta Compton*, is released by N.W.A.

2001 The hip-hop political action group, Hip-Hop Summit Action Network, is founded by Russell Simmons.

1992 Dr. Dre's album *The Chronic* is released; it redefines West Coast rap.

2006 The Smithsonian Institute National Museum of American History announces the creation of a new hip-hop exhibition scheduled to open in three to five years.

Sean Combs crosses the finish line of the 2003 New York Marathon. He had pledged to run the race in order to raise money to help New York City's schools. Although some people thought it was a publicity stunt, Puffy's effort and exhaustion were real.

◄1►

A Good Run

Sean Combs, also known as P. Diddy, had been running for miles. He had trained for weeks to run in the 2003 New York City **Marathon**, and his heart and mind were set on reaching the finishing line. But now that he was out there running for real, he wondered if his body would give out.

P. Diddy was not a professional athlete. He was a successful hip-hop artist, record producer, and **entrepreneur** who had earned tens of millions of dollars during his career. He had decided to run the New York Marathon, a grueling 26.2-mile long race, as a charitable fundraiser—a way he could use his influence to help people who were less fortunate.

Combs was troubled by the state of public schools in New York City. His own children attended excellent private schools, but he knew that most people in the Big Apple could never find the money for the expensive tuition these schools charged. He felt the best way to improve education for all children in New York was to raise money for the public school system. On his website, P. Diddy explained why he wanted to run:

> **"** Every child needs a high-quality education and proper healthcare in order to prepare for the 'Marathon of Life.' On Sunday, November 2, I am going to run the New York City Marathon and truly take this cause to the streets of NYC by showing the world that we have the determination and commitment to make a positive change for our children's future. Through 'Diddy Runs the City,' I am hoping that people become more aware of the health and educational needs that face the children of New York City. **"**

The hip-hop star had many rich and powerful friends who agreed to contribute if he completed the marathon. Actors Jennifer Lopez and Ben Affleck promised to donate $78,000 to his cause, while the rapper Jay-Z pledged $25,000. Even the mayor of New York, Michael Bloomberg, contributed $10,000. Such major corporations as Nike, McDonalds, and Pepsi also agreed to sponsor Diddy's marathon run.

Under Pressure

P. Diddy was thrilled with the response from his wealthy friends. However, the more money he raised, the more pressure he felt. Many stories about his benefit run appeared in newspapers, magazines, and television shows during the weeks leading up to the marathon. If Diddy could not make it to the finish line, it would be a huge embarrassment. He worried about letting himself—and the children of New York—down.

The marathon became a popular race at the first modern Olympic Games in 1896. Running such a race is not easy, and many runners participate simply for the accomplishment of covering the distance. The race is named after a village in ancient Greece called Marathon. In 490 B.C. a messenger was ordered to run to Athens and report the outcome of a battle between the Greeks and Persians. According to legend, a young man named Pheidippides ran the entire distance, more than 20 miles. When he arrived at Athens, Pheidippides shouted, "Rejoice, we conquer!" then dropped dead of exhaustion. Modern marathon runners train intensively to keep from injuring themselves when they attempt the long run.

Diddy said that he had been inspired to run the New York City Marathon by Oprah Winfrey, who had run a marathon herself in 1994.

"It has been a goal that I've wanted to achieve for a long time," the hip-hop star said on Oprah's program. "And so you doing it has been a great inspiration." He even vowed to beat her time!

As the race started, thousands of people milled around P. Diddy. During the first few miles, he smiled and waved at television cameras, which followed his progress even though he was far behind the leaders. But his cheerfulness would not last.

By publicizing the "Diddy Runs the City" event, Combs was able to raise $2 million in pledges. However, this also placed pressure on him to complete the race. Failure would disappoint all the kids who could have benefited.

Reaching the Finish Line

As P. Diddy neared the halfway point of the race, it seemed like the finish line was still impossibly far. "It's gonna be a rough one," he had told reporters. "Probably around the 13th mile, I'll really need your support." He was right. His chest burned as he gasped for air, his abdomen was tortured by cramps, and his legs felt like rubber. He

New York City mayor Mike Bloomberg, Sean Combs, Caroline Kennedy, and city schools chancellor Joel Klein pose with a large check for $2 million. Half of that money was donated to fund libraries and technology in city schools.

feared he would have to drop out. But then he saw that he was not alone. Children had begun to run next to him, shouting, clapping, and cheering him on. They reminded him why he was there and why it was so important for him to finish.

Combs staggered across the finish line in 4 hours and 18 minutes. He even managed to beat Oprah's 1994 time by 15 minutes. "The kids wouldn't let me stop," he told the *New York Daily News* after the race. "I was running for them, and they wouldn't let me stop." To those who claimed he had run the race just to draw attention to himself, he said simply: "Twenty-six miles is not a publicity stunt."

P. Diddy raised over $2 million that day. Half of that amount was given to New York City's public school system, and the rest was donated to other various worthy causes, such as the Children's Hope Foundation and Daddy's House Social Programs. The hip-hop star had surpassed even his own expectations and was thrilled with the results. "It's an honor and a blessing," he exclaimed, "to do something good for the city."

Sean Combs and his mother, Janice, celebrate the tenth anniversary of Bad Boy Entertainment in 2004. Because of the strength and support she gave to her son while he was growing up, Combs named his mother as owner of Bad Boy.

2

Inborn Ambition

The artist who would become known as P. Diddy was born Sean Combs on November 4, 1970. His family lived in Harlem, an African-American neighborhood in New York City. The neighborhood had once been culturally vibrant, but by the time Sean was born, the area had gone into a decline.

Two of a Kind

Sean's parents were Melvin and Janice Combs. Melvin was both a public servant who worked for the city's board of education and a New York City cab driver. Janice had a modestly successful modeling career. It seems to have been their love of all things glamorous and **flamboyant** that drew the young people to one another. "My mom . . . was like the fly girl of the neighborhood," Sean would later say, "and my pops was the fly guy of the neighborhood. That's how they got together."

Though life in Harlem could be rough, Melvin and Janice worked hard to provide a relatively stable life for Sean and his younger sister, Keisha. Unfortunately, Janice didn't know that between his legitimate jobs, Melvin was also dealing drugs and running small-time gambling operations. The extra money from these illegal pursuits allowed the couple to buy an expensive Mercedes-Benz and wear the newest, flashiest clothing. Janice soon had little Sean modeling along with her at fashion shows. As a result of that exposure, Sean was chosen to appear in a print ad for Baskin-Robbins ice cream. "As soon as that spotlight hit me, I just embraced it," he later recalled.

When Sean was just a toddler, his father's double life caught up with him. On January 26, 1972, Melvin was shot in the head while sitting in his car near Central Park. Janice didn't want to lie to her children, but she did not want to tell them about their father's illegal activities. She told them that Melvin had been killed in a car accident. Sean would not know the truth about his father's death until he was a teenager.

After Melvin's death, Janice began working long hours to provide for her two children. Sean went to live with his grandmother, Jessie, in a **government-subsidized** Harlem housing project called Esplanade Gardens. He credits Jessie's strong faith in God and her loving nature as important influences in his early life. Sean's mother and grand-mother wanted him to know there was a world beyond Harlem, so they took advantage of such programs as the Fresh Air Fund, in which families who live in the country host city children for the summer. One year, Sean spent a few months living with a family that was **Amish**. On their farm, Sean learned about their simple, old-fashioned way of living.

Janice was eventually able to buy a home in the upscale community of Mount Vernon, New York, but she didn't move her children there right away. She believed that a few more years in Harlem would give them strength they could rely on for the rest of their lives, and she didn't want them to become spoiled. Sean later said he respected this decision. In Harlem he learned to stand up to bullies and fight for what was rightfully his. He learned to be a survivor.

Time for a Change

In 1982 Sean and his sister finally joined their mother in Mount Vernon. Though the adjustment was not easy and took some time, for the most part Sean was happy about the move. In Mount Vernon there was not the crime, overcrowding, and drug culture of Harlem. Sean could relax and think about his future, rather than just try to get by from day to day. Janice made it clear that he was to apply himself to his studies and avoid any troublemaking. "Go to school and pay close attention to your teachers if you want to be a millionaire," she told her

Sean Combs never forgot the place where he grew up. When it came time to shoot ads for his Sean John clothing line, Combs chose Harlem as the location for filming. Here he talks to neighborhood kids that have gathered around the staging area.

children. Sean was enrolled at Mount St. Michael Academy, a private Catholic high school.

In Harlem Sean had grown up with a new form of music: hip-hop. Artists such as Kool Herc, Run-D.M.C., and KRS-One were among his favorites. Not only did he have their records, he would sometimes sneak into their live shows to see them in action. Now in Mount Vernon, he often felt alone in his musical taste. His white classmates listened to heavy metal bands like Van Halen and Aerosmith. Still, Sean had many friends at school and enjoyed playing on the football team. It was on the field, puffing his chest out to intimidate opponents, where he acquired the nickname "Puffy."

Sean sometimes referred to his new environment as "money-earnin' Mount Vernon," and the mentality rubbed off on him. After school and on weekends, he'd take any job he could. For a while he worked at an amusement park. His peers might laugh or even taunt him about the job, but he didn't care. He wanted to make money. He wanted to accomplish something. He wanted to leave his mark on the world.

It was around this time that Sean began to be very curious about his father. He still went to Harlem to visit his grandmother, and the stories her neighbors told about Melvin Combs were often different from the stories his mother had told him. Sean knew that his father had made a lot more money than a city worker or a cab driver could possibly earn, and he knew his father had a reputation for driving an expensive car and wearing fine clothing. Sean suspected his father had been involved in illegal activities and that there was more to his death than what he'd been told. At age 14 he went to the local library and dug up some old newspaper stories about the incident. There, he learned the truth. Sean later told interviewers that he was not angry, because he knew his mother had lied to protect him, but that he felt better knowing the real story.

College Life

Sean did well in school, and his mother was proud and happy when he applied for college and was accepted at Howard University in Washington, D.C. Howard had been founded in 1867 as a place where former African-American slaves could get an education. Sean felt honored to attend a college with such a rich and meaningful history. He tried to concentrate on his studies. However, the music industry

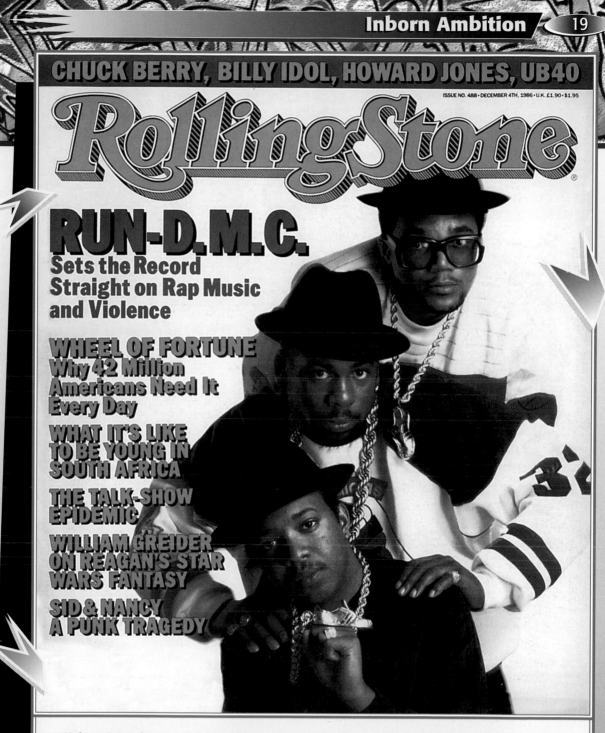

CHUCK BERRY, BILLY IDOL, HOWARD JONES, UB40

ISSUE NO. 488 • DECEMBER 4TH, 1986 • U.K. £1.90 • $1.95

Rolling Stone

RUN-D.M.C.
Sets the Record Straight on Rap Music and Violence

WHEEL OF FORTUNE
Why 42 Million Americans Need It Every Day

WHAT IT'S LIKE TO BE YOUNG IN SOUTH AFRICA

THE TALK-SHOW EPIDEMIC

WILLIAM GREIDER ON REAGAN'S STAR WARS FANTASY

SID & NANCY A PUNK TRAGEDY

This 1986 issue of *Rolling Stone* features Run-D.M.C., one of the first acts that made hip-hop a mainstream phenomenon. The combo from Hollis, Queens, was one of Sean Combs's favorite hip-hop groups while growing up.

seemed to be calling him more than ever. During his high school years, he had appeared as a dancer in videos for such artists as Fine Young Cannibals and Babyface, and he missed the excitement of show business.

Sean began calling himself Puff Daddy and formed a company with a classmate at Howard, Deric Angelettie. Deric was a popular deejay who shared Puffy's love of hip-hop. In an interview with author Ronin Ro, he fondly remembered the young Puff Daddy:

Puff Daddy performs with backup dancers at the 2005 MTV Video Music Awards. In college, Puffy made a name for himself with his innovative dance steps, and his earliest work in music was as a backup dancer.

> **" When Puffy came, he was a very flashy guy. . . . He'd be in the middle of the floor doin' all the new dances. And his style of dress was a little more colorful, bolder. Everyone took notice of this cool, overconfident dude. "**

Together, Sean and Deric decided to become party promoters, and they were immediately successful. It seemed as though everyone in Washington, D.C.—and many people from New York, also—wanted to attend Puffy's parties. For two years, Puffy and Deric went to class by day and threw parties at night. Howard University itself hired them to host their homecoming ball in 1989. Everyone was shocked when 4,500 people showed up and an entire city block had to be cordoned off. This kind of success could not go unnoticed for long. Soon, Puffy had attracted the attention of some of the biggest names in show business.

Rapper Heavy D, who first put Puff Daddy in contact with Uptown executive Andre Harrell, poses with Combs at the 2000 premiere of *Shaft*. Heavy D & the Boyz were the first group Harrell signed to Uptown.

3

Climbing the Ladder of Success

Puffy tried to settle down to his studies, but with each party or appearance in a video, he became more anxious for stardom. He saw friends forming hip-hop groups and becoming successful and felt he simply could wait no longer for his own fame. He had the necessary connections; he just needed to use them.

An Important Meeting

An old friend of Puffy's from Harlem, Heavy D, had made a name for himself rapping with his group, Heavy D & the Boyz. Two of their albums, *Living Large* (1987) and *Big Tyme* (1989), had been hits for the hip-hop label Uptown Records. Uptown had been founded by Andre Harrell, an African-American entrepreneur. Harrell and Combs were alike in many ways. Both men had boundless optimism and a positive attitude, and each believed he was destined for greatness. In Harrell, Puffy saw everything he wanted to be. He asked Heavy D to arrange an introduction.

Harrell liked Puffy's ambition and decided to give him a job as an intern at Uptown Records. Interns work like regular employees, but they usually get paid in school credit instead of cash. Many people work as interns for record companies, but very few are able to make a career in the business. Puffy knew that to succeed he would have to work hard. If the other interns at Uptown Records worked 8 hours a day, he would work 10 or 12. If Harrell asked him to pick up a tape from another studio, Puffy would run all the way. During meetings, he would take detailed notes that he could study later.

Harrell was impressed with Puffy's commitment to the job. When the head of Artists & Repertoire (A&R) at Uptown resigned in 1991, Harrell tapped Combs to fill the position. Puffy accepted and, much to his mother's disappointment, dropped out of college.

The High Life

The days of scraping by as a poor student were over for Puffy. In his new job, he would be responsible for finding and developing unknown singers and performers for Uptown Records. The job paid well, and Harrell moved Puffy into his luxurious New Jersey mansion. Puffy had his own suite, nice cars to drive, and a pool in which to relax. After work a limo would pull up in front of the Uptown offices and take Harrell and Combs to an expensive restaurant for dinner, then out to clubs for a night of partying.

At first Puffy was content to do his job and keep a low profile. After observing others in the music business, however, he realized that having a higher profile and attracting attention would help him to succeed at bringing new talent to the label. He had been brash and bold at Howard and was sure that a flashy image would be a great promotional tool. He hoped Harrell would be pleased with the media attention. "I've never let anyone down who was willing to take a chance on me," Combs told *Paper* magazine.

One of Puffy's first big projects was promoting an R&B quartet from North Carolina called Jodeci. The group's name was mixture of the names of brothers Joel "JoJo" and Cedric "K-Ci" Hailey and brothers Dalvin and Donald "DeVante Swing" DeGrate. The members of Jodeci were barely out of their teens and did not know much about show business. They came from a small town and thought they could succeed by imitating slick, sophisticated groups like Boyz II Men and Color Me Badd. But as their producer, Puffy had different ideas. The marketplace was already flooded with those kinds of color-coordinated, polished groups. He did not believe people would pay for more of the same.

Puffy decided to take Jodeci in a completely different direction, and Harrell agreed with his decision. The Jodeci guys would not be untouchable idols. They would look like guys that one might see on the streets of any city—regular guys that fans could identify with. Combs

Through his association with Andre Harrell and Uptown Records, Puff Daddy was ushered into the world of luxurious living. In this 2005 photo, Harrell (at left) and Combs are pictured here attending a fashion show in New York City.

asked his girlfriend, Misa Hylton, to help him dress the members of Jodeci. She put them in trendy but casual clothing and accessories, such as brightly colored baseball caps, sweatshirts, and low-slung, baggy jeans. Many friends and acquaintances were skeptical, but the look was a hit, especially with teenagers. This was an image they could relate to.

The album cover for Jodeci's *Forever My Lady* shows the group in their carefully crafted urban street look. Along with the trend-setting fashion sense that Puffy suggested, the boys had a musical sound that was unique.

Puffy influenced the group musically as well. The R&B music scene had become lifeless, he felt. Everything fresh was happening in hip-hop, but hip-hop had an edge that most R&B fans weren't interested in. With Jodeci, Puffy tried to integrate the two genres and made his first foray into extensive use of **sampling**. This technique requires permission from the original artist, and Puffy was able to convince high-profile performers to sell him the rights to use pieces of their songs. Although some people did not think the new sound would work, Puffy again proved he was right. Jodeci's 1991 debut album, *Forever My Lady*, and their first single of the same name raced to the top of the R&B charts. Jodeci became a **crossover hit**, and their album went double platinum, meaning it sold over 2 million copies.

A Girl Named Mary

Combs was pleased with Jodeci's success, but he knew that a producer needed more than one hit to prove himself. He wanted to make a follow-up album that would announce to the world that *Forever My Lady* was no fluke. And he didn't want to play it safe. He wanted to choose an artist who was as different from the fellows in Jodeci as possible.

In Mary J. Blige, Puffy found the perfect vocalist for his next project. As a young girl, Mary had started singing in her church choir to escape from her troubled home life. She had talent as a vocalist, and Mary's friends encouraged her to record herself singing at a **karaoke** booth in the Galleria Mall in White Plains, New York. Her mother passed the tape to a boyfriend, who played it for Uptown employee Jeff Redd. Ultimately, Mary J. Blige was signed to Uptown, and Combs was chosen to produce her first album and shape her image.

Puffy was excited to work with Mary, and she was grateful to be in the hands of someone so talented. However, she had a strong temperament of her own and sometimes rebelled against Puffy's ideas for her image. Mary didn't have enough money to move out of her family's bad neighborhood, and she felt arrogant parading her wealth and success in front of her neighbors. Yet Combs insisted that she present a certain image at all times. This combination of poor urban living and expensive accessories came to be known as "ghetto fabulous," and Mary was crowned its queen.

These problems were forgotten—at least temporarily—when the first album they made together, *What's the 411?*, was released on July 28,

Puff Daddy poses with one of his stars, Mary J. Blige, at the second annual Hip-Hop Summit Action Awards dinner in 2004. Mary was just a girl from the projects until her demo tape made its way to Uptown and Puffy.

1992. It became an almost overnight sensation. *What's the 411?* sold 2 million copies, and its first single, "Real Love," hit number one on the R&B charts and number six on the pop charts. Just as he had with Jodeci, Puffy had made liberal use of samples from other artists' records in making Mary's album. This was becoming his trademark, and for the time being the critics raved about it. They also raved about Mary, comparing her to such vocal legends as Billie Holiday and Aretha Franklin.

Puffy's work as a producer made Mary J. Blige a phenomenon. Her rise to fame was sometimes even more than she could handle. She was expected to perform in front of large crowds, including the 2003 NFL Kickoff Concert depicted here.

Good Intentions Gone Bad

Just as Puffy was gaining attention in the music business, he was affected by his involvement in a horrible tragedy. In 1991, he helped plan a fundraiser for a group called AIDS Education Outreach. The "Heavy D and Puff Daddy First Annual Celebrity Basketball Game" was scheduled to take place December 27, 1991, at the Nat Holman Gymnasium at New York's City College. Combs lined up members of Jodeci, Boyz II Men, and A Tribe Called Quest to perform. Unfortunately, more than 5,000 people showed up at a venue that had a capacity of only 2,700. The excited crowd grew restless before the concert. When the crowd pushed forward, nine people were crushed and smothered

Sean "Puffy" Combs talks to reporters in 1998 after testifying at a lawsuit over deaths at a 1991 City College concert. The courts decided that in addition to Puffy, many other parties were to blame for the accidental deaths.

against the arena doors. What should have been a night of revelry turned into a terrible tragedy.

Though others had been involved with the planning, Puffy was the event's most prominent spokesman, so local and national media came down hard on him. News reports claimed he had been irresponsible and incompetent. College officials said that, "[we] had never been informed that rap stars would be involved in the game," and that "the event wouldn't have been permitted if [we] had." Some saw racism in these remarks; after all, 11 fans had been crushed to death at a concert of the white British band The Who in 1979, but no one had blamed rock music for the deaths.

The Manhattan district attorney's office investigated the incident and found that there was plenty of blame to go around. Its report criticized the police for not properly controlling the crowd, student organizers for not informing City College that there would be a large turnout, the college for not providing enough security, emergency medical services for slow response, and Sean "Puffy" Combs for questionable fund-raising practices. No one in the AIDS service community seemed to know what the AIDS Education Outreach Program was. There was no record of any charity under that name registered anywhere in the country, and none of the funds raised had been set aside. Some critics concluded that the game had been billed as a "charity event" as part of a marketing ploy.

For the first time in his life, Puffy faced failure, and it was a failure that had cost the lives of nine people. Suddenly, old friends and business associates did not have time to take his calls. Andre Harrell asked him to stay away from the Uptown offices until the media storm blew over. Everyone but his mother Janice, his girlfriend Misa, and his lawyers seemed to be against him. Combs later said that only his faith in God got him through that difficult time.

The tragedy at City College affected Puffy greatly, and he suffered from a deep depression. But he would not let the setback destroy his career. He hadn't yet achieved the greatness that he always felt destined for.

4

Trouble at the Top

Sean Combs spent several months out of the limelight, dealing with feelings of depression over his role in the tragic accident, before he was able to return to work. He soon bounced back, however. Puffy would achieve great success over the next few years, but he continued to be dogged by violence and tragedy.

Big Changes

In 1993 Puffy began working with a rapper named Christopher Wallace, who performed under the name Notorious B.I.G. or Biggie Smalls. Biggie had been a small-time drug dealer in Brooklyn, but he had a talent for creative raps. After being released from jail on a drug charge, he recorded a tape of some songs. Biggie did not think much would come of his rapping, but the tape wound up in Puffy's hands. Biggie's rich, polished vocal style and intense, detailed lyrics impressed the producer.

When the two first met, Puffy was surprised to find that the man who was so articulate behind the microphone was closed-mouthed and modest. "When I first met Biggie, he was real quiet and shy," Puffy told *MTV News*. Biggie was also smooth and **charismatic**, and at six foot three inches tall and over 300 pounds, no one could miss him. They agreed to work together, and the collaboration would change both of their lives.

Rapper Notorious B.I.G. (also known as Biggie Smalls) poses at the 1995 *Billboard* Music Awards. Biggie quickly became Puffy's good friend and Bad Boy's biggest star. The Brooklyn rapper's debut, *Ready to Die*, was hugely successful.

Puffy soon began to slowly introduce Biggie to rap fans. First, he had him record a song for a movie soundtrack. Next, Biggie contributed vocals to a Mary J. Blige album. Soon, the two were working on songs for Biggie's first album.

Personally, things were also going well for Puffy in 1993. He was excited when his girlfriend Misa gave birth to their first child, a son named Justin. But soon, Puffy would experience a crushing professional disappointment.

Parting from Uptown

In 1993, Puffy suffered a painful break with Uptown Records, when his mentor Andre Harrell fired him from the label. Uptown executives felt Puffy was too rebellious and too full of himself, and Harrell decided that he had no choice but to let Puffy go.

The decision may have been just business for Harrell, but for Puffy it was a nightmare. He cried for days. Puffy later said he felt like he was going through a divorce, and told *Rolling Stone* magazine that he "wanted to jump off a building."

Others in the music industry recognized that the young producer had great talent, however, and soon after he was fired large record labels had begun offering him jobs. But despite the high-paying job offers, Combs was not really sure what he wanted to do. He considered starting his own record label, but even after all the years as Harrell's **protégé** he was nervous about running a business on his own.

Things changed after he received a call from Clive Davis, the founder of Arista Records. Davis was something of a legend in the music industry, having discovered and nurtured such artists as Janis Joplin, Bruce Springsteen, and Whitney Houston. When Davis called Puffy to discuss his future, he did not talk about money like other record company executives. Instead, Davis seemed to understand what Puffy was going through. He asked about his music and his creative vision. Combs appreciated this conversation, and it may have helped him decide what he wanted to do with his future. Less than two months after parting with Uptown, Puffy formed his own record label, Bad Boy Entertainment, and signed a $15 million distribution contract with Clive Davis and Arista Records.

Davis was ecstatic about the deal with Puffy. The Arista head told *Billboard* magazine, "He has a feel for the street and combines it with an unusual grasp of what can best bring it to the marketplace."

Music industry legend Clive Davis, the founder of Arista Records, is pictured with Whitney Houston, whom he signed to a recording contract when she was a teenager. Davis had an eye for talent, and supported Puffy's dream of forming his own rap label.

Although a few people complained that Puffy was too inexperienced to succeed, Combs simply ignored the critics and went about his work. "People are going to say what they will," he told *Newsweek*, "particularly when you're young, black, and successful."

On His Own

To thank his mother Janice for standing by him through the tough times, Sean named her the official owner of Bad Boy Entertainment. To remind himself of the awesome responsibility now on his shoulders, he hung a sign in the lobby of his new office that said, "Life Is Not A Game."

Puffy got down to business right away, signing and releasing albums for hot new artists like rapper Craig Mack and singer Faith Evans. He brought Biggie Smalls to Bad Boy and completed his debut album, *Ready to Die*. It became Bad Boy's first major hit when it was released in September of 1994, selling more than 4 million copies and winning several awards. Combs was pleased with the success and happy for Biggie, who had become a close friend.

Although Mary J. Blige stayed at Uptown Records, Puffy took over as her manager and continued to produce her songs. He had a hand in nearly every track on her second album, *My Life*, which was a major critical and commercial success. *My Life* went on to sell 3 million copies.

Puffy spent a lot of time and energy on Mary's career, but he was also busy signing other artists and groups to Bad Boy Entertainment, including 112 and Total. He was also in great demand as a producer. Combs collaborated with many hip-hop and R&B stars, including Lil' Kim, TLC, Mariah Carey, Boyz II Men, SWV, and Aretha Franklin.

A Deadly Feud

Unfortunately, Sean Combs's great success would soon bring him enemies. In Los Angeles, a man named Marion "Suge" Knight had built a successful recording company called Death Row Records. Death Row specialized in the hip-hop sound known as **gangsta rap**, a hardcore musical style that used the rough vocabulary of Los Angeles gangs and idealized violence. Knight's lineup of artists included the rappers Tupac Shakur and Snoop Doggy Dogg and the influential producer Dr. Dre.

Puffy did not consider Death Row to be in competition with Bad Boy. For the most part, Puffy's label concentrated on a type of hip-hop music that was far more positive and upbeat than the hardcore rap that Knight's label was turning out. The two men were even casual friends, occasionally meeting to discuss the music industry and their experiences. And Puffy's most famous artist, Notorious B.I.G., was friendly with Knight's biggest artist, Tupac Shakur. These relationships would be shattered, however, by a shocking incident on November 30, 1994.

That night, Tupac was in New York to attend his sentencing trial on a legal matter. He had been asked to collaborate with an artist named Little Shawn at a studio on Times Square while he was in town. As they

Death Row recording artists Tupac Shakur (left) and Snoop Doggy Dogg (center) pose with the founder of Death Row Records, Marion "Suge" Knight. Los Angeles-based Death Row helped popularize the "gangsta rap" sound of the west coast.

entered the studio lobby, two armed men approached Tupac and his friends. They demanded money, then shot Tupac five times.

Tupac survived the attack, but afterward he came to believe that the robbery had not been a random event. The shooting *was* suspicious: one of the men was already inside the building when Tupac arrived, and at that hour visitors had to be buzzed into the lobby. Puffy, Biggie, and Andre Harrell were in an upstairs studio when the attack occurred, and Tupac came to believe they had set him up to be killed. Tupac later gave an interview to *Vibe* magazine accusing Puffy and Biggie of masterminding the shooting. But no formal charges were ever brought in the shooting, and there was no evidence that Biggie or Puffy had been involved.

A wheelchair-bound Tupac arrives at court on December 1, 1994, the day after being shot five times in a New York recording studio. Tupac believed that Notorious B.I.G. and Puff Daddy had been behind the attack.

The relationship between Bad Boy and Death Row turned into what some magazines called the East Coast–West Coast rap feud. Throughout 1995 and 1996, Tupac and Biggie expressed their anger and contempt for each other in their lyrics. There were also several run-ins involving rappers from Bad Boy and Death Row. In September 1996, the feud turned deadly. Tupac was ambushed while riding in a car with Suge Knight, and the rapper died from his wounds a few days after the attack.

Six months later, Biggie and Puffy attended a party together in Los Angeles. When the party ended, they left to go to another party. Biggie and Puffy got into separate cars, along with some of their friends. They didn't get very far, however. When Biggie's vehicle stopped at a red light, a black car pulled up alongside and a man fired seven bullets into Biggie's body. Mortally wounded, the rapper slumped over in his seat as the car containing the gunman zoomed away.

Puffy witnessed his good friend's murder. "I jumped out of my car and ran over to his," Combs later told the *New York Daily News*. "I was saying the Lord's Prayer and Hail Marys. I was begging God to help him out. I was touching him and talking to him in his ear." However, the 24-year old rapper was pronounced dead at a Los Angeles hospital.

Remembering a Friend

Puffy was devastated by the death of his best friend. He called for an end to the East Coast–West Coast conflict, saying, "Christopher Wallace, a.k.a. Notorious B.I.G., you will always be in my prayers, along with all of the urban youth whose lives were ripped away by senseless violence." He also promised to take care of Biggie's family.

Just two weeks after Biggie's murder, his second album, *Life After Death*, was released. The album quickly shot to the top of the *Billboard* chart, and the first single off the album, "Hypnotize," likewise hit number one. Eventually, some 10 million copies were sold. The music received critical praise also. In *Rolling Stone*, reviewer Anthony DeCurtis lauded both Biggie and Puffy, who had produced the album. "Together they constructed a sprawling, **cinematic** saga of the thug life," he wrote.

Puffy next recorded a song of his own to honor the memory of his friend. "I'll Be Missing You" also featured Biggie's wife, singer Faith Evans. The song was a smash hit, and touched many people. However, when a few people complained that the song was exploiting Biggie's tragic death, Puffy promised that any money he made from the hit would be put in a trust for Biggie's mother and children.

Faith Evans and Sean Combs announce the release of their tribute to Biggie Smalls, "I'll Be Missing You." Some critics accused Bad Boy of trying to profit from Biggie's death, but proceeds from the hit went into a fund for Biggie's kids.

A Force in the Music World

On July 22, 1997, Bad Boy Entertainment released *No Way Out*, Puff Daddy's first album. It immediately became a number-one hit. Combs explained the title of the album in *Spin* magazine: "At times, I feel like I'm trapped inside a movie starring me, but I'm not the director, and I don't know what the scene is, nothing." *No Way Out* featured a group of Bad Boy performers known as the Family, including Jay-Z, Lil' Kim, the L.O.X., and other artists. In addition to "I'll Be Missing You," the single "Can't Nobody Hold Me Down" also reached the number-one spot.

The critics were not kind to *No Way Out*. Most felt that Puffy's continued use of samples had grown old, and they were not impressed with his lyrics and song subjects. Combs tried to be true to the life he'd led, but a few critics implied he was a wimp because he hadn't rapped like a gangsta. Still, Puffy's millions of fans and soaring record sales more than made up for their harsh reviews.

Puff Daddy holds up his Grammy won in 1998 for Best Rap Album for his debut release, *No Way Out*. He also won a Grammy that year for Best Rap Performance by a Duo for "I'll be Missing You" with Faith Evans.

During the late 1990s, Puffy continued to produce albums for some of the biggest stars in the music business. One hit was Mariah Carey's 1997 album *Butterfly*, which had sales of over 235,000 its first week and debuted at number one on the *Billboard* pop chart. Puffy was credited with adding a hip-hop edge to Carey's music.

Puffy could also turn unknown artists into stars. One of these was a rapper named Ma$e, whom Combs had signed to Bad Boy in 1996. Ma$e had been a hardcore rapper for years, but Combs tried to fit him into the glamorous, upscale Bad Boy mold. In 1997, Ma$e's first album, *Harlem World*, was another hit, and he soon became Bad Boy's premier star. Clearly, Puffy had become one of the most important and powerful figures in the music industry.

Personal Life

Puffy continued experiencing ups and downs in his personal life. After he and Misa Hylton broke up, Combs began dating a fashion model named Kim Porter. On March 30, 1998, Kim gave birth to Sean's second child, a boy the couple named Christian.

However, Kim and Sean did not remain together long after the baby was born. Puffy had been introduced to an up-and-coming dancer and actress named Jennifer Lopez in 1996, when she appeared in the video for his hit song "Been Around the World." Lopez was ambitious and wanted a music career. In 1999, she and Combs began a much-publicized relationship. He also helped produce her hit debut album in 1999, *On the 6*.

Jennifer Lopez and Sean Combs attend the 2000 MTV Video Music Awards. After breaking up with Kim Porter, Combs started a relationship with Lopez. Intense publicity and the strain of Puffy's trial for a nightclub shooting incident may have contributed to their breakup.

5
Controversy and Charitable Works

n 1998 Combs wanted to change Bad Boy's image and make the label more hardcore, so he began working with a rapper named Shyne. Shyne had run with gangs in Brooklyn, been shot several times, and spent time in a juvenile detention facility. Friends warned Combs that the rapper was dangerous, but he ignored them.

Puffy's friends had been right. On December 27, 1999, Combs was partying at a nightclub with Jennifer Lopez and Shyne when shots rang out. Combs and Lopez tried to leave, but their car was stopped and searched by police. They found a gun, and Puffy was arrested for weapons possession. Shyne was caught outside the club holding a handgun, and he was also arrested.

Combs hired celebrity attorney Johnnie Cochran to defend him at his trial. It was a media circus. **Paparazzi** mobbed the courthouse every day. Prosecutors asserted that Puffy had tried to get his limousine driver, Wardel Fenderson, to claim the gun as his and take the rap. Fenderson refused and told the authorities the same story over and over: he had nothing to do with the gun or the shooting and hadn't even been inside the club.

On March 16, 2001, the trial ended with Combs acquitted of all the charges. However, it had been a publicity nightmare. Bad Boy's record sales were steadily falling. Top stars were leaving the label, and Puffy's follow-up to *No Way Out*, the 1999 album *Forever*, had been both a commercial and critical disappointment. Perhaps because of the pressure of the trial, Lopez broke up with Puffy in February 2001.

Ups and Downs

It was time for a new start, and, symbolically, Combs decided to change his name. "No more Puff Daddy," he told MTV in March 2001. "It is going to be changed to straight P. Diddy. You could call me P., or Diddy, or P. Diddy."

P. Diddy started branching out into other areas of the entertainment world. In 2002 he starred in the MTV program *Making the Band 2*. "I have been creating stars since I was 19, and this show will give insight into what it takes to be at the top," he said in a press release. "I'm excited to be working with MTV and doing what I love to do—create and nurture new talent." Though the reality show got good ratings, the band he formed in front of millions of viewers failed to hit the charts. Never one to give up easily, P. Diddy signed on for *Making the Band 3*, this time trying to popularize an "all-girl" pop group. Again, the public did not respond as he had hoped.

Combs had better luck on the big screen, garnering good reviews for his work in the Academy Award–nominated 2001 film *Monster's Ball*. A reviewer for the film industry newspaper *Variety* wrote, "rap star Combs impresses by avoiding the slightest hint of melodrama." While some critics thought he might even get an Academy Award nomination for Best Supporting Actor, when Oscar season rolled around, his name was not on the list of nominees.

In 2004 P. Diddy tried stage acting, and tickets sold swiftly when he appeared on Broadway in a revival of the play *A Raisin in the Sun*. Though reviews were mixed, the show's producers knew that the name "Sean Combs" would bring in people regardless. "This is all happening because of him," producer David Binder said of the spectacular box

A poster for a 2004 Broadway production of *A Raisin in the Sun*. Combs was one of the show's stars, playing Walter Younger, a character originally played by legendary actor Sidney Poitier. Combs's performance drew generally good reviews.

office numbers. "Sean brings them in and that crosses a lot of different lines. So many different kinds of people can connect to him." P. Diddy's celebrity friends Oprah Winfrey, Beyoncé Knowles, and Russell Simmons were there to support him on opening night. Critic Howard Kissel of the *New York Daily News* reported that Combs "showed plenty of stage presence."

New Areas of Success

Spectacular triumphs always seemed to heal the wounds of P. Diddy's disappointing failures. When Arista Records stopped distributing Bad Boy releases in 2002, P. Diddy simply remade Bad Boy as an independent record company and kept going. In 2005 he signed a deal with Warner Music Group that gave the record company a 50 percent stake in Bad Boy Records in exchange for a reported $30 million. "This has ensured for the next couple of years that we have the right financial backing, the right financial structure, the right partners to remain a force in the music industry," P. Diddy said.

Combs's clothing line, Sean John, has been an undisputed smash hit, raking in millions of dollars since its launch in 1998. In fact, his design sense got him nominated as Menswear Designer of the Year in 2002, 2003, and 2004 by the Council of Fashion Designers of America. He took home the 2004 award for Best Menswear. The motto of the Sean John line, "It's a Lifestyle," reflects P. Diddy's belief that his music, business ventures, and personal style are intertwined.

Combs never stops looking for ways to expand his fashion creativity, and in 2006 he even launched a designer fragrance, *Unforgivable*. Within just a few months, *Unforgivable* became the best-selling men's fragrance in the United States, bringing in an astounding $1 million dollars a week. It was yet another triumph for the multitalented mogul. Naturally, a fragrance for women is not far behind.

P. Diddy has also made an impact in the restaurant business. In 1997 he opened a restaurant called Justin's in New York. Justin's, which is named after his eldest son, offers a tasty combination of American Southern cuisine, soul food, and Caribbean dishes. The atmosphere is elegant but not stuffy. And P. Diddy insists that he's just as serious about the restaurant business as he is about everything else he does: "I'm not just a talker. I open up a restaurant and I keep it open." He has opened additional Justin's restaurants in cities like Atlanta and Detroit, and intends to make it into a national chain.

The management team for Sean John Fragrances is invited by John Thain, the CEO of the New York Stock Exchange, to NYSE to celebrate the success of *Unforgivable*, the number one men's fragrance in the country.

In 2006 P. Diddy's love of good food also inspired him to produce another reality TV project, *Celebrity Cooking Showdown*, for the NBC network. It featured three gourmet chefs teaching nine celebrities how to cook in a fiercely competitive boot camp–type setting. "People love seeing celebrities under pressure," P. Diddy said in a statement, "and with this show, if you can't stand the heat, you better get out of the kitchen."

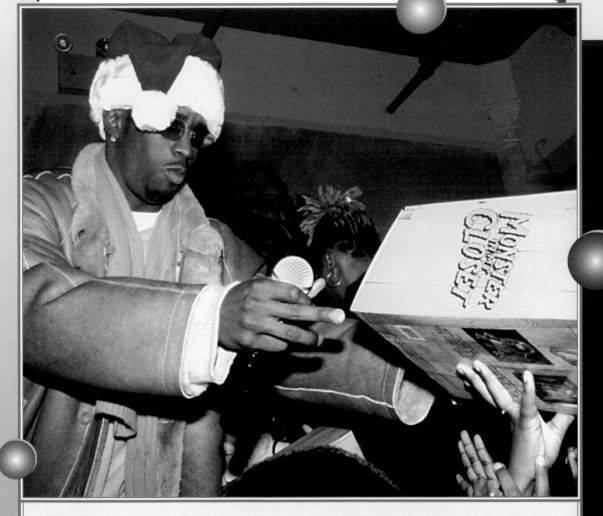

Wearing a festive Santa hat, Sean Combs hands out presents at Russell Simmons's Rush Philanthropic Arts Foundation party in December 2000. The foundation was created to introduce the arts to disadvantaged young people in New York City.

Giving Back

In the 21st century, Sean Combs intends to give back to the community that has supported his dreams for so long. His charitable foundation Daddy's House Social Programs, which he established in 1995, creates educational programs for disadvantaged children, teaches teens about financial management, and helps high school seniors find the right college. Another organization, Daddy's House International Travel Groups, give inner-city students a chance to visit other cultures, study Third World trade, and gain a global perspective on political and economic problems.

In addition to running his charities, Diddy loves to play Santa every holiday season. At last count, he was personally delivering gifts to over 3,000 children a year. Children's hospitals and foster homes are filled with cheer when P. Diddy and crew arrive to make the holidays just a little better for sick and lonely kids all over the New York area.

When Hurricane Katrina hit the Gulf Coast, P. Diddy rushed to help the victims. He and fellow rapper Jay-Z, who has own clothing line called *Roc-A-Wear*, banded together to donate their designer clothing to those left homeless by Katrina. They also made a joint gift of $1 million to the American Red Cross, to be used to help victims relocate and start over. P. Diddy told the *New York Post*, "These are my people. I urge all our fellow artists and Americans to answer the call."

Concerned Citizen

In 2004 P. Diddy announced a voter-awareness campaign called Citizen Change. He explained that it would be nonpartisan, which meant that it would not endorse any particular political party but would urge average citizens to get involved in the democratic process. Combs felt that there were certain groups in the country who were not being well represented by politicians and had therefore given up on the idea that they could change things through voting. He wanted to inspire everyone to believe that they could make a difference. "We cannot hold politicians accountable if we don't hold ourselves accountable," he said.

Combs thought he could sell the public on voting the same way he sold them on an album or an item of clothing. He decided on the motto "Vote or Die" for his new campaign and plastered it across thousands of T-shirts. His goal, he said, was to "Make politics fashionable. . . . People use fashion to create a statement all the time." The target of the campaign, P. Diddy told reporters at a press

Seagrams CEO Edgar Bronfman Jr. and Sean Combs work on a house as part of a Habitat for Humanity project in September 2005. The organization was constructing new homes to replace houses in the South that had been destroyed by Hurricane Katrina.

conference, was the "42 million Americans age 18 to 30 that are eligible to vote on November 2." He warned that if all Americans did not exercise their voting rights, the future of the country could be negatively affected: "If I'm scaring you, then good, 'cause that's how serious that is."

As usual, P. Diddy had plenty of celebrity friends who were happy to help him get the word out. 50 Cent, Leonardo DiCaprio, Snoop

On MTV's *Total Request Live* in 2004, Combs promotes a get-out-the-vote campaign for the presidential election. With the slogan "Vote or Die," he hoped to make voting trendy and popular among young people who might not otherwise turn out at the polls.

Sean Combs and his son Justin attend the 45th Annual Grammy Awards at Madison Square Garden. Despite all that he has already accomplished, Combs still intends to be a major influence on the hip-hop world.

Dogg, Jay-Z, and Ashton Kutcher are just some of the many stars who lent their names to his cause. Combs attended both the Democratic and Republican national conventions in 2004 and gave television interviews to as many news outlets as he could.

It is impossible to determine how much of an impact Combs's campaign had. However, the overall voter turnout during the 2004 election was 60 percent, up from 55 percent in the 2000 presidential election. The average turnout for voters under 30 was up approximately 10 percent in 2004.

Producer, rapper, actor, fashion designer, **restaurateur**, marathoner—it seems there's nothing P. Diddy can't do when he sets his mind to it. The only question is: what can he possibly do next? Combs told *Vox* magazine: "I've still got a long way to go to make the type of impact I want to make."

1970   Sean Combs is born on November 4 in New York City.

1972   Sean's father, Melvin Combs, is shot to death on January 26.

1982   Janice Combs moves her children to Mount Vernon, New York.

1987   Sean Combs graduates from Mount St. Michael Academy and begins attending Howard University.

1988   Meets Uptown Records founder Andre Harrell.

1991   Andre Harrell names Puffy head of Artists & Repertoire at Uptown. Puffy produces his first album for the group Jodeci, the hugely successful *Forever My Lady*. Nine people die of asphyxiation on December 27 at a basketball event organized by Puffy.

1992   Produces Mary J. Blige's album *What's the 411?*, which becomes an overnight sensation after it is released on July 28.

1993   Begins working with Biggie Smalls (The Notorious B.I.G.); after being fired from Uptown Records, starts Bad Boy Entertainment and signs a distribution agreement with Clive Davis of Arista Records.

1994   First child, a boy named Justin, is born to Misa Hylton; Bad Boy releases the Notorious B.I.G.'s first album, *Ready to Die*, on September 13; rapper Tupac Shakur is shot in a New York recording studio on November 30, but survives.

1995   The bitter East Coast-West Coast rap feud develops between Bad Boy Entertainment and Death Row Records.

1996   Tupac is shot and killed in Las Vegas during September.

1997   In March, Biggie Smalls is shot and killed in Los Angeles; *No Way Out*, Puff Daddy's first album as a performer, is released on July 22; Puffy performs his hit "I'll Be Missing You," a tribute to Biggie Smalls, with Faith Evans and Sting at MTV's *Video Music Awards*.

1998   Second child, a boy named Christian, is born to Kim Porter on March 30; Puffy debuts his clothing line, Sean John.

1999   On August 24, Puff Daddy's second album, *Forever*, is released; arrested after a shooting at a New York nightclub on December 27.

2001 On March 16, Puffy is acquitted of weapons charges in the nightclub shooting; changes name to P. Diddy; receives critical acclaim for his performance in the film *Monster's Ball*.

2002 Stars in *Making the Band 2* on MTV.

2003 Successfully completes the New York City Marathon on November 2, raising $2 million for charity.

2004 Makes his Broadway debut in *A Raisin in the Sun* on April 26.

2006 Introduces his designer fragrance, *Unforgivable*, in January.

Albums
As Puff Daddy
1997 *No Way Out*

1999 *Forever*

As P. Diddy
2001 *The Saga Continues*

2002 *We Invented the Remix, Vol. 1*

Top Ten U.S. Singles
1997 "Can't Nobody Hold Me Down" (featuring Ma$e) #1

"I'll Be Missing You" (featuring Faith Evans & 112) #1

"Mo Money, Mo Problems" (Notorious B.I.G. featuring Puff Daddy & Ma$e) #1

"It's All about the Benjamins" (with The Family) #2

1998 "Been Around The World" (with The Family) #4

"Come With Me" (featuring Jimmy Page) #4

"Lookin' At Me" (Ma$e featuring Puff Daddy) #8

1999 "All Night Long" (Faith Evans featuring Puff Daddy) #9

"Satisfy You" (featuring R. Kelly) #2

2002 "I Need A Girl (Part One)" (featuring Usher & Loon) #2

"I Need A Girl (Part Two)" (with Ginuwine featuring Loon, Mario Winans, & Tammy Ruggieri) #4

"Bump, Bump, Bump" (with B2K) #1

2003 "Shake Ya Tailfeather" (with Nelly & Murphy Lee) #1

2004 "I Don't Wanna Know" (Mario Winans featuring Enya and P. Diddy) #2

Grammy Awards

1998   Best Rap Album, *No Way Out*

       Best Rap Performance by a Duo or Group, "I'll Be Missing You"

2004   Best Rap Performance by a Duo or Group, "Shake Ya Tailfeather"

Other Awards

2004   Named Best Menswear Designer by the Council of Fashion Designers

Books

Bowman, Elizabeth Atkins. *Sean "Puffy" Combs.* New York: Chelsea House Publications, 2003.

Cable, Andrew. *A Family Affair: The Unauthorized Sean "Puffy" Combs Story.* New York: The Ballantine Publishing Group, 1998.

Chang, Jeff, and DJ Kool Herc. *Can't Stop Won't Stop: A History of the Hip-Hop Generation.* New York: St. Martin's Press, 2005.

Lommel, Cookie. *The History of Rap Music.* New York: Chelsea House Publications, 2001.

Perry, Imani. *Prophets of the Hood: Politics and Poetics In Hip-Hop.* Durham, N.C.: Duke University Press, 2004.

Quinn, Eithne. *Nuthin' but a "G" Thang: The Culture and Commerce of Gangsta Rap.* New York: Columbia University Press, 2004.

Ro, Ronin. *Bad Boy: The Influence of Sean "Puffy" Combs on the Music Industry.* New York: Simon & Schuster, 2001.

Rose, Tricia. *Black Noise: Rap Music and Black Culture in Contemporary America.* Middletown, Conn.: Wesleyan University Press, 1994.

Simmons, Russell. *Life and Def: Sex, Drugs, Money, + God.* New York: Crown Publishers, 2001.

Watkins, S. Craig. *Hip Hop Matters: Politics, Popular Culture, and the Struggle for the Soul of a Movement.* Boston: Beacon Press, 2005.

Web Sites

The official website of P. Diddy's label, Bad Boy Entertainment.
www.badboyonline.com

P. Diddy's official website.
www.diddyonline.com

The website of P. Diddy's clothing line, Sean John.
www.seanjohn.com

Rock on the Net has a very informative page about P. Diddy.
www.rockonthenet.com/artists-p/puffdaddy_main.htm

Yahoo!'s artist page for Biggie Smalls, contains a biography and music clips.
http://music.yahoo.com/ar-259391-The-Notorious-BIG

Amish—a Christian religious sect that lives in a simple way and avoids the use of most modern technology.

charismatic—possessing great personal charm.

cinematic—typical of the style in which movies are made.

crossover hit—a song of a particular genre that becomes popular among listeners who normally would not listen to that type of music.

entrepreneur—a person who establishes new businesses in order to make a profit.

flamboyant—flashy, loud, and showy.

gangsta rap—a hardcore, tough musical style that emerged in the late 1980s and became popular during the 1990s. Gangsta rap songs are often about violence, drug use, or mistreatment of women.

karaoke—a machine that plays instrumental music selections so the user can provide his or her own vocals. Often, karaoke machines will be attached to a display that gives the user the lyrics and visual cues for how to sing.

marathon—a race of 26.2 miles.

paparazzi—aggressive photographers who follow celebrities, hoping to get candid photos which they can sell to magazines.

protégé—a young person who receives guidance, training, and support from somebody who is older and more experienced.

restaurateur—a person who owns a restaurant.

sampling—taking a short musical phrase from one song and using it in another recording.

subsidized—a grant or donation, often from the government or a charitable organization, that helps to pay for something.

acting career, 46–48
AIDS Education Outreach, 30–31
Angelettie, Deric, 20–21
Arista Records, 35, 48

Bad Boy Entertainment, 14, 35–43,
  45–46, 48
"Been Around the World" (Combs), 43
Big Tyme (Heavy D & the Boyz), 23
Biggie Smalls. *See* Notorious B.I.G.
Billboard Music Awards, 34
Binder, David, 46, 48
Blige, Mary J., 27–29, 35, 37
Butterfly (Carey), 43

"Can't Nobody Hold Me Down"
  (Combs), 41
Carey, Mariah, 43
charity work, 8–13, 50–55
Citizen Change, 51–53
  See also charity work
City College concert deaths, 30–31, 33
Cochran, Johnnie, 45–46
Combs, Janice (mother), 14–17, 31,
  36–37
Combs, Keisha (sister), 16
Combs, Melvin (father), 15–16, 18
Combs, Sean ("Diddy")
  acting career, 46–48
  albums, 41–42, 46
  arrest of, for weapons possession,
    45–46
  awards won by, 42
  at Bad Boy Entertainment, 35–43,
    45–46, 48
  charity work, 8–13, 50–55
  childhood, 14–18
  and City College concert tragedy,
    30–31, 33
  dancing career, 20–21
  and East Coast-West Coast rap
    feud, 37–40

family life, 35, 43–44, 54
at Howard University, 18, 21, 24
name change (to P. Diddy), 46
and the New York Marathon, 8–13
and "Puffy" nickname, 18
relationships, 10, 26, 31, 35, 43, 44–46
Sean John clothing line, 17, 48
Sean John Fragrances, 48–49
sons (Justin and Christopher), 35,
  43, 54
at Uptown Records, 22–29, 31, 33–35

Daddy's House Social Programs, 13, 51
  See also charity work
Davis, Clive, 35–36
Death Row Records, 37–40
DeCurtis, Anthony, 40
DeGrate, Dalvin, 24
  See also Jodeci
DeGrate, Donald ("DeVante Swing"), 24
  See also Jodeci
"Diddy Runs the City." *See* New York
  Marathon
Dr. Dre, 37

East Coast–West Coast rap feud, 37–40
Evans, Faith, 37, 40–41, 42

Fenderson, Wardel, 46
Forever (Combs), 46
Forever My Lady (Jodeci), 26–27
Fresh Air Fund, 16

gangsta rap, 37–38
Grammy Awards, 42

Hailey, Cedric ("K-Ci"), 24
  See also Jodeci
Hailey, Joel ("JoJo"), 24
  See also Jodeci
Harlem, 15–17, 18
Harlem World (Ma$e), 43

Harrell, Andre, 22–23, 24, 31, 35, 38
Heavy D, 22–23
Heavy D and Puff Daddy First Annual Celebrity Basketball Game, 30–31, 33
Hip-Hop Summit Action Awards, 28
Hylton, Misa, 26, 31, 35, 43
"Hypnotize" (Notorious B.I.G.), 40

"I'll Be Missing You" (Combs), 40–41, 42

Jay-Z, 10, 41, 50
Jodeci, 24–27
Justin's (restaurant), 48

Kissel, Howard, 48
Knight, Marion ("Suge"), 37–38, 40
Knowles, Beyoncé, 48
Kool Herc, 18
KRS-One, 18

Life After Death (Notorious B.I.G.), 40
Lil' Kim, 41
Little Shawn, 37
Living Large (Heavy D & the Boyz), 23
Lopez, Jennifer, 10, 43, 44–46
L.O.X., 41

Mack, Craig, 37
Ma$e, 43
Making the Band 2, 46
Monster's Ball, 46
MTV Video Music Awards, 20, 44
My Life (Blige), 37

New York Marathon, 8–13
No Way Out (Combs), 41–42
Notorious B.I.G., 33–35, 37–40

On the 6 (Lopez), 43

P. Diddy. See Combs, Sean ("Diddy")
Porter, Kim, 43, 44
Puff Daddy. See Combs, Sean ("Diddy")
"Puffy" Combs. See Combs, Sean ("Diddy")

A Raisin in the Sun, 46–48
Ready to Die (Notorious B.I.G.), 34, 37
"Real Love" (Blige), 28
Redd, Jeff, 27
Ro, Ronin, 20–21
Run-D.M.C., 18, 19

sampling, 27, 28, 42
Sean John (clothing line), 17, 48
Sean John Fragrances, 48–49
Shakur, Tupac, 37–40
Shyne, 45
Simmons, Russell, 48, 50
Snoop Doggy Dogg, 37–38

Thain, John, 49
Total, 37

Unforgivable (fragrance), 48–49
Uptown Records, 22–27, 31

voting awareness campaign. See Citizen Change

Wallace, Christopher. See Notorious B.I.G.
What's the 411? (Blige), 27–28
Winfrey, Oprah, 10–11, 13, 48

Kelly Wittmann is the author of two children's history books, *Explorers of the American West* and *The Rediscovery of America,* and another children's book about Botswana. She currently lives in Chicago.

Picture Credits

page

2: KRT/NMI

8: UPI/Monika Graff

11: KRT/Nicolas Khayat

12: Richard B. Levine/PS

14: Ronald Asadorian/Splash News

17: Paul Cunningham/Ace Pictures

19: NMI/Michelle Feng

20: Zuma Press/NMI

22: Zuma Press/Nancy Kaszerman

25: Mitch Gerber/Star Max

26: NMI/Michelle Feng

28: Zuma Press/Aviv Small

29: KRT/Olivier Douliery

30: UPI/Ezio Petersen

32: KRT/Olivier Douliery

34: Zuma Press/Jane Caine

36: A. Turner/J Records/NMI

38: NMI/Death Row Records

39: KRT/David Hanschuh

41: UPI/Ezio Petersen

42: Gary Hershorn/Reuters

44: UPI/Laura Cavanaugh

47: Splash News

49: Sean John Fragrances/NMI

50: UPI/Ezio Petersen

52: Zuma Press/Nancy Kaszerman

53: Zuma Press/Nancy Kaszerman

54: KRT/Lionel Hahn/Nicolas Khayat

Front cover: Billy Farrell/PMC/SIPA
Back cover: AFP/Anna Zieminski